THE NAMES OF JESUS

The story of Jesus' birth based on
Isaiah 9:6–7; 60:1–6; Matthew 2:1–12;
and Luke 1 and 2, for children.

Written by Lisa M. Clark
Illustrated by Ian Dale

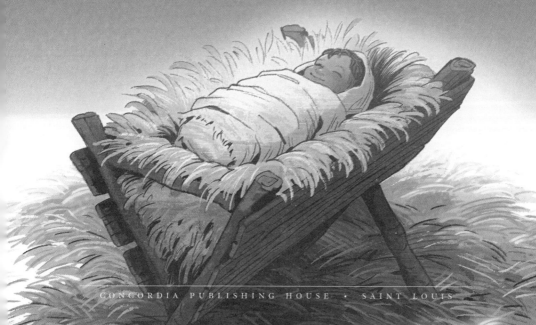

CONCORDIA PUBLISHING HOUSE · SAINT LOUIS

In ancient days so long ago, the Lord proclaimed His plan:
The Son of God would someday come and be the Son of Man.
He told Isaiah to write down some special names to learn
So we would know our Savior and the freedom He would earn.

So Wonderful this Counselor would be for all below;
Our Mighty God would come and live with us, His grace to show.
Our Prince of Peace would put an end to all our sin and pain
Till we would everlasting see our Father rule and reign.

The people waited for so long for to meet this promised One
Until an angel shared the news of God the Father's Son.
The angel said to Mary, "You are favored by the Lord,
For you will bear the Son of God, whom angels have adored.

"The baby you will love and raise will have a special name,
For Jesus means 'the Lord will save,' and this will be His fame.
He is the Son of David, and His rule will never end."
This King will live and die and rise and then He will ascend.

This Mary was engaged, betrothed, to marry a good man.
His name was Joseph, and he did not know the Father's plan.
So, in a dream, an angel came to tell the happy news.
The angel said, "Immanuel will be a name to use.

"Immanuel means 'God with us,' and God will live with you.
So, Joseph, care for Him, and know the Lord will see you through."
This special couple would provide for this awaited child,
And in this baby, God and people would be reconciled.

Elizabeth and Zechariah both were very old,
But they received amazing news from what an angel told.
They also would expect a son, and he would show the way;
This prophet would proclaim the One who takes our sins away.

The Most High Lord and Lamb of God were names they heard and said,
For Jesus would die for all sin and rise up from the dead.
So, John grew up and preached the Word, that God was coming near,
And all who turned from sin and shame could meet Him without fear.

The promised day had come at last: the Son of God was born!
Some shepherds watched their sheep at night,
    just waiting for the morn.
To their surprise, the darkened skies were filled with angel light
As they proclaimed that Christ the Lord was born that very night!

Both Simeon and Anna were excited for the grace
That came through Jesus, and they both could see His little face.
"Salvation!" Simeon proclaimed; "I've seen Him with my eyes!"
"Redemption!" Anna, too, rejoiced, to see this blest surprise.

And even still the news was shared by God's prophetic star,
So, Wise Men traveled untold years with greetings from afar.
"Where is the King?" They looked and found the One who came for all.
They worshiped Jesus, giving gifts, this ruler still so small.

So many names are given to our Savior, Jesus Christ;
Each one can teach us of the One who once was sacrificed.
He died for all and rose again and someday will return.
So, as we wait and worship Him, these many names we learn.

LAMB OF GOD ◇ REDEEMER ◇ THE SON OF GOD

PRINCE OF PEACE ◇ EVERLASTING FATHER

WONDERFUL COUNSELOR ◇ MIGHTY GOD

SON OF MAN ◇ IMMANUEL ◇ MOST HIGH LORD

Dear Parents:

Names can be special. This was true in Bible times, and it is especially the case for Jesus. As God the Father kept reminding people of His promise to send the Messiah, He used special names for this Promised One so people would learn about Jesus. When Jesus was born, more names were shared by angels and in song to tell the world more about this promised Child.

As you read this book with your child, talk about the names of people in your family. Share stories behind the names you have. Do your names have special meanings? Does anyone have a name that has been passed down in the family?

Jesus means "the Lord saves." Immanuel means "God with us." Christ means "the Anointed One." Jesus was anointed, publicly shown as God's chosen Savior, to be with us in order to live, die, and rise to save us from our sins and to give us new life in His name.

We have our own names. Because of Jesus, we are given the name of "child of God." In Baptism, the name of the Father, Son, and Holy Spirit is placed on us, as God claims us as His own.

As you learn more about Jesus' birth and His names, think about how these names tell us about His great love for us. Say a prayer to Him, thanking Him for the forgiveness He has earned. Consider ending the prayer with "In Your name we pray. Amen."

The Author

JESUS